HEART to HEART

Yours daily effective prayers that gets limitless results

ALAIN LEA

Heart to Heart: Homologeo. Copyright © 2020. Alain Lea.

All rights reserved. No part of this publication may be reproduced, distributed, or transmitted in any form or by any means, including photocopying, recording, or other electronic or mechanical methods, without the prior written permission of the publisher or author, except in the case of brief quotations embodied in critical reviews and certain other non-commercial uses permitted by copyright law. For permission requests, write to the publisher, addressed "Attention: Permissions Coordinator," at the address below.

ISBN: 978-1-952806-04-9 *(paperback)*
ISBN: 978-1-952806-07-0 *(eBook)*
ISBN: 978-1-952806-06-3 *(audio)*

Christ In All Nations, Inc
info@christinallnations.org
P.O Box: 588
Granger, IN 46530
www.christinallnations.org

Cover design: CIAN Publishing Team

Page layout by: CREATIVEDZINE-99designs Inc.

Scripture quotations taken from the New King James Version (NKJV).
Copyright © 1982 by Thomas Nelson. Used by permission. All rights reserved.

Printed in the United States of America

Acknowledgment

First and foremost, I want to thank my Papa, my good, sweet, and lovely Father, for pouring out His wisdom from within. Each of these prayers come from a place of intimacy I cannot explain in words. You satisfied me with Your fullness each day and I thank You. I have experienced Your guidance day by day and I cannot thank You enough. I appreciate Your help. Allow your children to experience what I have experienced while writing these words. Blow, touch, speak audibly, appear, reveal, open their eyes. You did much more than I can say, let him/her experience You like never before.

I would like to express my special appreciation and thanks to my mother, Doumbe Endene Marie. You have been a tremendous mentor to me. I thank you for encouraging me when no one believed in me, even myself. You taught and allowed me to love the people around me, regardless of their color, ethnicity and religion. Your advice on both my personal life as a young man as well as my participation in the ministry of our Lover, Jesus Christ, have been invaluable.

I want to thank Christ In All Nations Team for believing in me as a person and leader: Apostle Beth Thomas, Chantal Reymond, Minister Joe Alvarado, Mark Irvin, Prophet Diboundje Yvan, Minister Binam Christele, Prophet Simon Issa, Prophet Eudes, to name a few; thank you for serving nations in love, even through hardship or challenges. I also want to thank you for your brilliant comments and suggestions.

I would especially like to thank God for doctors, nurses, and nurse aids who are fighting every single day to take care of people who are fighting the COVID-19 and any other medical condition. Even those who will not be able to read this book, all of you have been there to help save lives as much as you were able to.

A special thanks to my entire family. Words cannot express how grateful I am to all of you for all the sacrifices that you have made on my behalf. Your prayer for me was what sustained me thus far. Thank you for supporting and encouraging me throughout this experience. You guys are always cheering me up.

> **To Him who lavished every blessing heaven has upon us in Christ!**

Preface

Heart to heart: an intimate conversation or discussion. **Synonyms of 'heart to heart' include** a 'tête-à-tête'; a French phrase that means, 'A cosy chat; a one-to-one private conversation in an environment of total freedom.

For you to experience the true victory of salvation, you need to be able to have a heart to heart conversation with the triune God; in which you can fully express your feelings, personal challenges or problems.

Get ready to experience the kind of relationship that God has always intended between Him and you. Get ready for a heart-to-heart journey with Our Father in Heaven, Jesus Christ, and The Holy Spirit.

Before starting your journey of heart to heart confessions to the Father, through Jesus Christ, please make sure you read the important thoughts shared in this book.

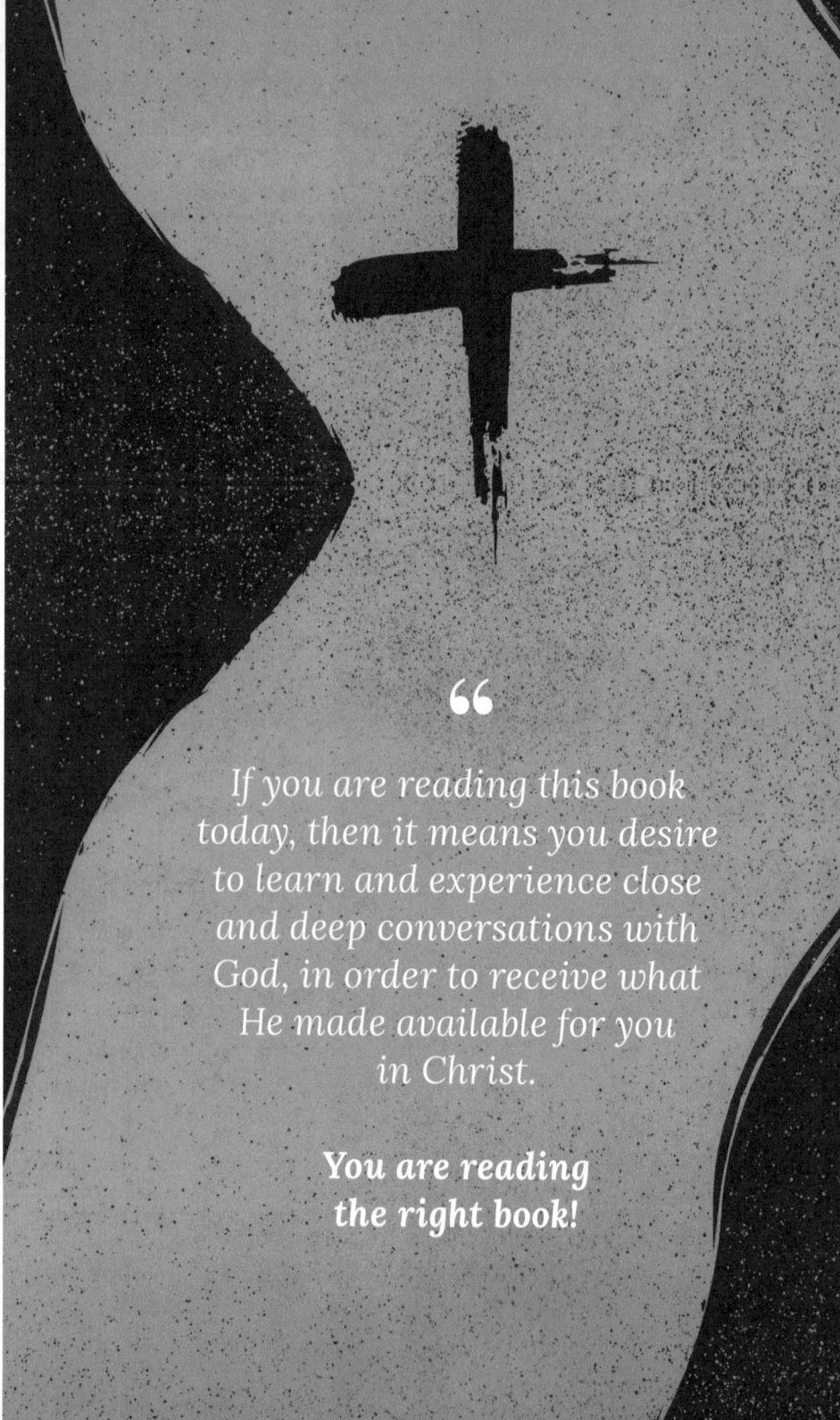

Table of Contents

Acknowledgment	ii
Preface	iv
Important Thoughts on Prayer	11
Why You Have Not Received What You Asked For?	12
Confession	16
Daily Prayer of Thanksgiving	17
Plea for Awakening	18
Prayer While in a Gaze	19
Prayer for Peace	20
Contemplation Prayer	21
Prayer for Direction	22
Heart To Heart Talk	23
Prayer for When you Feel Unworthy	24
Prayer to Be a Blessing to Someone Else	25
Intercession for the Broken-Hearted	26
Confession: Seeing the Father Through Jesus	27
Prayer of Perseverance	28
Prayer for Charging Your Angels	29
Prayer for Self-Control	30
Prayer for Alignment	31
Intercession for Friends	32
Prayer for Healing of the Soul	33
Intercession for the Troubled Hearts	34
Prayer of a Repentant and Grateful Heart	35
Prayer from a Re-Acclimated Heart	36

Prayer to Counter Evil / Darkness	37
Prayer for Inner Rest	38
Prayer Against Fear	39
Prayer when Sad and Depressed	40
Acknowledge Jesus as My All	41
Prayer from a Worried Heart	42
Prayer When Feeling Inadequate	43
Gratitude in the Midst of Pain	44
When in Need of God's Provision	45
Participating in the Faith of Jesus	46
Prayer for Confidence	47
Prayer for Heavy Hearted	48
Prayer for Hope and Trust	49
Prayer of Content Gratitude	50
Heart To Heart Talk	51
Prayer for Restoration in Relationships	52
Awakening of Souls to the Knowledge of Jesus	53
Prayer for a Suffering Friend	54
Prayer for Physical Healing	55
Prayer to Find a Life Partner	56
Intercession for Someone's Awakening	57
Prayer for Strength	58
Prayer for Employment in Trying Times	59
Prayer for a Friend Who is Moving	60
Prayer for Inner Stillness	61
Fellowship with The Holy Spirit Regarding Ministry	62
Thanksgiving for Being Blessed	63
Prayer for Wisdom	64

Prayer for Identity	65
Heart To Heart Talk	66
Declaration of Belonging	67
Affirmation of My Position in Christ	68
Confession of the Measure of Christ	69
Confession of Spiritual Awakening	70
Intercession for Healing Our World	71
Prayer for Intimacy	72
Thanksgiving for Restoration	73
Acknowledging Jesus Christ	74
Gratitude for Insight	75
Prayer to Start the Day	76
Prayer from a Heavy Heart	77
Intercession for My Country and City	78
Prayer to Manifest Sonship	80
Heart To Heart Talk	81
Heart To Heart Talk	82
Heart To Heart Talk	83
Important	84
My Prayer for you	86
From God	87
Conclusion	88
The Ultimate Invitation	89
About the Author	92
Available on Amazon	93
Books Coming Soon	96

IMPORTANT THOUGHTS ON PRAYER

In the book of Matthew 6:5-15, the disciples of Jesus asked Him to teach them how to pray. His answer was unexpected. He started by confronting the misconceptions concerning prayer. In fact, Jesus started by countering false ideas and discussions on what prayer is not. He then taught His disciples the right way to pray. The religious system had become so hypocritical and fraudulent that the Lord had to undo what they commonly thought prayer was before He could effectively teach them what prayer really means.

While using this book, **I am not saying that only the written confessions contained in this manuscript are the only words to use when you pray; or that you won't get any results if you don't pray this way** but rather, the manuscript serves as a guide to align your words with God's thoughts. They will align your thoughts with what He intends for you and what He has spoken about you. The confessions you will be making will probably be very different from the way you usually commune with God, but rest assured that the Holy Spirit will help you to experience the wonderful freedom of heart to heart conversations in your relationship with our Father in Heaven.

WHY YOU HAVE NOT RECEIVED WHAT YOU ASKED FOR?

There is a lot of misguided understandings about prayer today, starting from the people on pulpits to the believer on the pews. All across the Christian world today, there are distorted assumptions and attitudes on prayer that are totally askew. So many believers wonder why they are not receiving what they prayed for, but the problem is simply infiltration of hypocrisy in the heart of the majority. Jesus taught that there is a right and a wrong way to pray:

And when you pray, you shall not be like the hypocrites. For they love to pray standing in the synagogues and on the corners of the streets, that they may be seen by men. Assuredly, I say to you, they have their reward.

[MATTHEW 6:5]

Most believers are not even aware of the hypocrisy of the heart when it comes to prayer. They assume because you are praying, nothing could be wrong. Quite the contrary is true. A lot and almost everything could be wrong in a prayer, when you love to pray for show, just like the hypocrites.

The heart attitude behind your prayer interests God much more than the actual words you say. Therefore, just because someone says, "*Our Father...*" and finishes with "*... in the mighty name of Jesus*" doesn't mean it is the right prayer.

Are you aware that it is impossible for anyone to impress God? Absolutely! If you do not have the proper motives, it does not matter what you do or don't do. You might ask, "But what is the right way then?"

Homologeo is a word that originates from the word homologos; which means, of one mind. from a compound of the base of *homoú*, which means 'together', and *légō*, which means '*speak* to a conclusion' – Homologeo is therefore properly defined as: *to voice the same conclusion,* i.e. *agree (confess)*; to profess (confess) because one is in full agreement; to align with (endorse) and to speak the same as.

Throughout this book, you will engage your thoughts, mind, and heart in the most honest and open conversations with God. You will find yourself praying in line with His heart. You will confess everything that He knows to be true about you, and you will find yourself aligning your thoughts with His. Above all, you will discover that love should always be the motivation of your **homologeo**.

God has already done everything you can possibly think or imagine. He did it all, once and for all, through Christ Jesus. Christ is God's full provision in you, for you and with you. Therefore, after the life, death and resurrection of Jesus Christ, it is not up to God to do anything for you anymore; you simply need to perceive what is yours, agree with what God says and receive the manifestation of it. It manifests effortlessly because it is already yours.

Therefore, when you pray, never think that you can twist God's arm to make Him do something your way. Prayer is like chatting with someone you dearly love; it is a heart to heart conversation based mostly on thanksgiving.

Do not turn your conversations with God into moments where you only want to inform Him on how bad your situation is. He knows before you open your mouth to speak, and He loves you more than you could possibly dream of loving yourself.

Instead of focusing on your unworthiness when you pray, thank Him for His goodness. You should not be afraid of God, He is your Father, your mother, brother, and everything else. He is always glad to hear from you. God wants you to be constantly aware of His love for you.

In light of who God is, no problem is that big. Prayer is worship; and worship is prayer. Fellowshipping with God in the midst of everyday life is an intimate relationship that should be developed over time.

If you have not yet experientially received *by grace* what you asked for, your self-faith cannot make Him do it. You see, the problem is not God's willingness or ability to manifest what He already gave us; rather, it is our ability to believe and receive what has already been given to us. Gazing into the beauty of God's glory, renders powerless and irrelevant anything that could try to distract your soul, mind and thoughts from His image and likeness in you. You will realize how insignificant your problems really are when you consistently keep your eyes on Jesus.

I advise you to read these thoughts several times until they become a part of you. They will become a mindset, that will shrink the problems around you so much, that it will be literally impossible for them to keep you anxious, sad, awake during nights, afraid or broken. You will be so conscious of God's love and care for you, that you will not even mistakenly think about what you do not have. God is faithful and He has already met your needs before they manifest in your present situation.

If you allow these words to detoxicate your belief system, you will be unstoppable.

CONFESSION

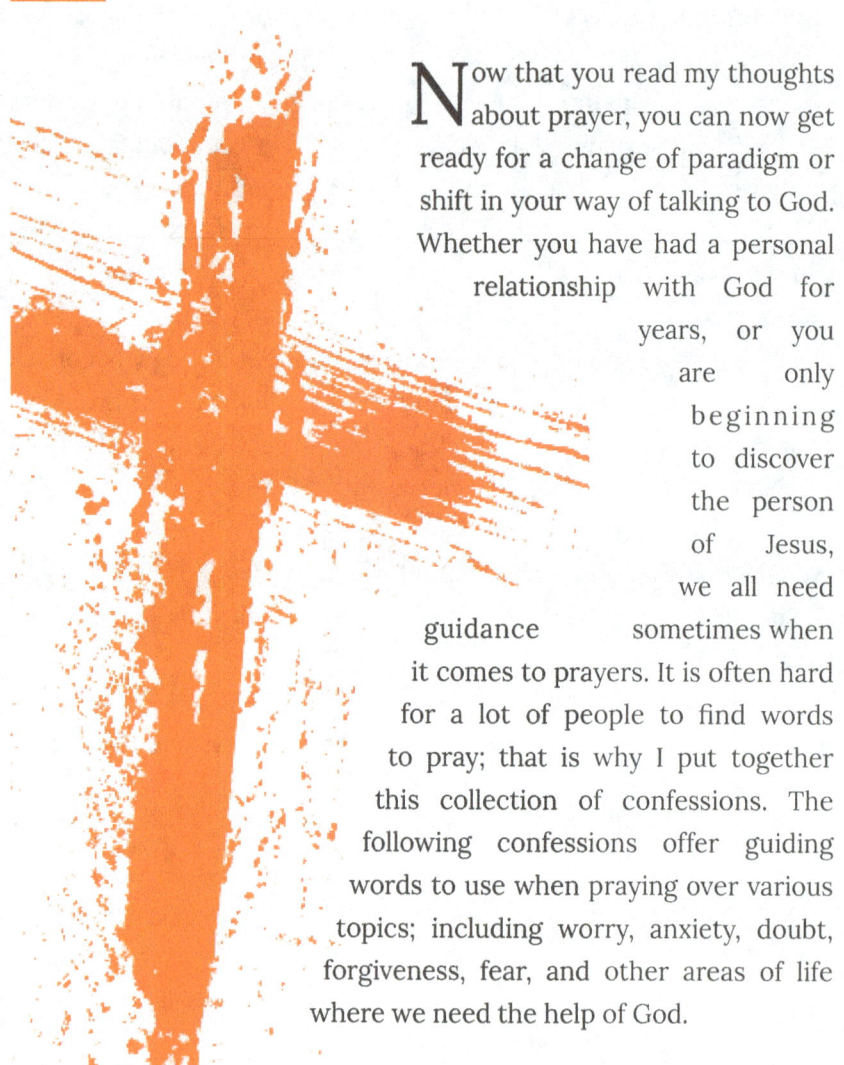

Now that you read my thoughts about prayer, you can now get ready for a change of paradigm or shift in your way of talking to God. Whether you have had a personal relationship with God for years, or you are only beginning to discover the person of Jesus, we all need guidance sometimes when it comes to prayers. It is often hard for a lot of people to find words to pray; that is why I put together this collection of confessions. The following confessions offer guiding words to use when praying over various topics; including worry, anxiety, doubt, forgiveness, fear, and other areas of life where we need the help of God.

Please use these prayers and allow the Holy Spirit to guide you, as you personalize your worshipful confessions to God the Father, through our Lord Jesus Christ.

Daily Prayer of Thanksgiving

Father, thank You for intervening in my life and allowing me to have a personal relationship with You.

Thank You for Your love for me today and forever.

Thank You for the blessings You have graciously lavished upon me and my family. Help us live in the consciousness of the fact that we are blessed to be blessings to anyone You put on our path today.

May I live a life of true joy as I see You at work through me and around me today. In Christ I pray.

Amen.

Plea for Awakening

Eternal and immortal Father, Lover of the human race, I am grateful because You have given me unlimited access to Your unearthly wisdom and revelation. I am thankful, my Father, that You qualified me to participate in the complete portion of the inheritance of the saints in the light by rescuing me from the dominion of darkness and relocating me into the kingdom of light, where the love of Your Son Jesus Christ rules. Your precious Holy Spirit constantly overwhelms my thoughts with an understanding of the magnitude of Your power in the finished work of Christ Jesus.

The eyes of my understanding are flooded with Your light and my heart is continuously in an enlightened state. Bathe my mind with Your love, so that I can fully understand in an experiential way the assurance that the presence of Your majesty brings in me; in the place of my deepest fears and doubts. This I pray in the name of Jesus Christ.

Amen.

Prayer While in a Gaze

Lord Jesus, beloved, eternal, and faithful Son of God incarnate, I thank You for continuously sharing Your knowledge of the Father's heart with me. You invade my pain with Your joy and peace. You searched out and silenced everything in me that could possibly keep me paralyzed and unable to be the ME that You have always known and shared Your unearthly assurance with. In the place of my deepest pain, You found all the broken parts of my heart, and soaked them with Your Father's love, until the beauty within me flooded my soul and manifested outwardly. Your precious Holy Spirit illuminates my heart with wisdom and revelation, so that I can know the deepest truth that are within Your Father's heart. His mysteries are revealed in me and to me, so that I continuously grow in a fuller, deep, intimate, and experiential knowledge of Him, through You. Daily, Your Spirit baptizes my soul in Your fullness.

Thank You, Lord Jesus Christ, for being my Lord and Saviour

Amen.

Prayer for Peace

Lord Jesus Christ, You are the beloved, eternal, and faithful Son of the Father in Heaven. I celebrate the fact that You tirelessly share Your knowledge of Your Father's heart with me.

Today, my heart is filled with chaos and confusion. I feel as if I am drowning in my circumstances and my heart is filled with fear and confusion. Lord, You came into my troubled heart once and for all with Your joy. You searched out the blindness in my heart and occupied it with Your unearthly tranquillity, in place of my greatest confusion. All the broken parts of my heart are now founded and bathed with Your Father's love. Thank You for giving me eternal salvation; and for always baptizing my soul, mind, heart and thoughts with Your unshakable peace.

Amen.

Contemplation Prayer

Lord Jesus Christ, beloved and eternal Son of the Father, Anointed of the Holy Spirit, incarnate, crucified, resurrected, and ascended Lord of all creation, You believe in me. With great delight, with the praise of my whole heart I acknowledge and agree that You have found me in my darkness and sin, laid hold of me and taken me down in Your death, freed me from sin and evil, quickened me with new life in Your resurrection, and lifted me up into Your Father's arms in Your ascension. All of me, and mine, every war-torn fragment, every fearful, unbelieving, broken part is in You, in Your Father, in the Holy Spirit. I rest in You, Jesus, lover of my soul, my Saviour, my Salvation, my Sovereign, my King, my Liberator, the Author and Finisher of my faith. You have included me in all that You are and all that You have in Your union and face-to-face communion with Your Father. You have included me in Your own anointing in the Holy Spirit. You have included me in Your victory over evil and wickedness, and in Your intercession at the Father's right hand, above all rule and authority in heaven and on earth. I am thankful that nothing can separate me from You, Your Father, and the Holy Spirit.

Amen.

Prayer for Direction

Precious and blessed Lord Jesus, You are the Lamb of God and Redeemer of God's image and likeness in me. You became what I thought I was so that I can rediscover who I have always been. Come into the weakest area of my emotions and feelings and help me not to lean on my own understanding; rather, to trust You in everything, my Lord, and to acknowledge You in everything I say, think and do so that You inspire me to make better choices of my words, thoughts and actions.

I open myself to be taught by Your Holy Spirit, to make intelligent decisions that are constructive and backed up by love. I ask You to preserve my thoughts and mind against any influence that could lead to choices, decisions or directions that are anti-love and contrary to what You pre-ordained for me. Light of the world, I give You permission to shine in my soul so that the wisdom of Your Spirit can be exhibited through me in all circumstances of my life (*Educational, Relationships, Career and Family*). Thank You for sharing with me Your Father's everlasting love today.

Amen.

Heart To Heart Talk

"

Let the Spirit Lead

Amen.

Prayer for Times When You Feel Unworthy

Lord Jesus, in Your courage, in the comfort of the personal presence of the Holy Spirit, and the unearthly assurance of Your Father's arms, I pledge all of me to Your service; to participate in Your ministry of liberation of our brothers and sisters. Reveal to me the agreements that I have made with evil and darkness, that I may turn away from these agreements by gazing on the beauty of Your Father's relationship with You, and that I may walk in every way in the glorious freedom of the children of God; in full agreement with the Holy Spirit, and in all His gifts.

I take my stand in You, Lord Jesus, and I thank You because my life, my body, my family, my sphere of influence, and my properties are blessed in You. Every spirit, power, prayer, curse, cover, idea and desire that is directed towards me that is not in full submission to You, Your Father, and the Holy Spirit will not affect me or whatever is mine in any way. I am valuable, worthy, qualified, accepted, good enough and precious in You. With great delight, with thanksgiving in my heart, I celebrate what You are for me, in me, to me and through me.

Thank you, Jesus Christ.

Amen.

Prayer to Be a Blessing to Someone Else

Eternal and Faithful Lord, Son of the Father incarnate, beloved King, Jesus. Thank You for having looked beyond my faults and for loving me unconditionally. When I fail to love others, in the light of what you did on behalf of the entire human race, I sincerely thank You for Your gentle mercy on me, due to my ignorance and blindness to the fact that You are love and You never change. You are the same yesterday, today and forever. Ignite in me that which I think I do not have: Faith, hope and love. Thank You because every form of darkness and evil that could possibly influence me, were rendered powerless once and for all on the Cross. Give me eyes to see the needs of the difficult people in my life, and show me how to meet those needs in the best way possible. Share with me Your own knowledge of the Father's heart, that I may know Your confidence, Your passion, Your joy and peace.

Thank You for continuously pouring out Your Spirit upon me, that I may be of service to You in the awakening of this generation to the good news of our adoption.

Amen.

Prayer for the Broken-Hearted

Lord Jesus, faithful, eternal, and beloved Son of the Father. I know You are with me, for me and in me right now. My heart is broken, and my mind is crushed right now, but I know You are my rescuer and my hope. Shower me with Your fondness, to heal the pain that I feel right now. My soul faints, but You are life and truth in me. You are the Lover of my soul, my Sustainer and Helper.

I am weak, but You are strong. Your Spirit, dear Lord Jesus, helps my gaze to be on You alone, and not on the dark cloud of despair I find myself in right now because You delight in me. I thank You for sharing with me Your own experience of Your Father's love. My soul is flooded with Your light, and my heart is in a peaceful and sound state right now. Soak my mind with Your Holy Spirit and let me see who I am in God through Your eyes, so that I may live with the accurate awareness and experiential knowledge of how loved and grounded I am in You. Thank You, dear Lord Jesus Christ.

Amen.

Confession: Seeing the Father Through Jesus

Lord Jesus, You are the Father's true Son, my faithful Saviour, and I am not ashamed of pouring my heart out to You. I am burdened and heavy-laden, I cannot continue to live a lie in my (**career, marriage, relationship, education, family, business, ministry**). I am tired, I feel as if I want to give up everything. I am at the end of my own ability to change or adjust any circumstance.

I tried to do it my way and I failed. I now admit that I need Your help. Grace my heart, my mind and soul with Your unwavering rest. Open my eyes that I might see what You have done for me. Pull the thread of my wrong headedness. I thank You because the circle of failure is undone. My guilt unravels into Your Father's forgiveness. Guide my heart to always yield to Your Spirit so that any presence of a hidden idol vanishes, until all I see is Your Father's face. I embrace Your knowledge and confidence of Your Father's heart. Pull me out of my abyss and show me the way to our Father's arms.

Amen.

Prayer of Perseverance

Precious Lord Jesus, Saviour of my soul, my salvation and saving act, Redeemer of the image and likeness of God in me. I celebrate and thank You for lovingly sharing with me Your personal experience of the Father's loving kindness. However, dear Lord, the hustles I am facing in my (**marriage, relationship, education, body, professional career**) keep me from feeling it.

I know I am never alone. I know that You will never forsake me, but the loneliness is terrifying. It is a battle rage that I cannot see. My soul is attacked with an invisible weapon. Give me Your eyes to see what is true about me so that I may consistently live in the consciousness of Your grace and peace manifested in me through Your indwelling. I am perseverant and courageous in You, Christ Jesus.

Thank you, Lord.

Amen.

Prayer for Charging Your Angels

Holy angels of God, you are faithful servants of God in my life. I appreciate your presence with me. I summon and command you today to annihilate any attempt of the power of darkness in my life, and to establish the Light of the blessed Trinity throughout my domain. I charge you to be the safeguards over my family and everything that is mine. Guard everything that I own (marriage, house, car, investment, relationship, business, etc.). Preserve me from all harm, danger, mal-intent, and any form of loss.

Today, as I am preparing to leave my house to go take care of what I have to do today, watch over my going out and my coming in. I charge you *holy angels* to go before me, with me and behind me. Protect every mode of transportation I will take; every building I am supposed to go to; everyone I am supposed to meet – even the people I did not plan to meet that I will meet. Prepare all my meetings and bless them with your presence so the outcomes will always be in line with God's plan for my life. Handle situations I am not aware of, for *God, my Father, charged you to watch over me, to keep me in all my ways. In your hands you will bear me up, lest I dash my foot against a stone.* In Christ I speak,

Amen.

Prayer for Self-Control

Lord Jesus, precious Lover of my being, in the light of my inclusion in Your death and resurrection, and in full agreement with the Holy Spirit, I believe and acknowledge that I should not see myself or anyone else the way we used to be when we were not aware of our true nature and identity. In You, I am a brand-new person. Forgive me for underestimating myself sometimes, through the negative and harmful words that I speak and think about myself, when things are not the way I expect them to be or look the way I want them to look.

I ask You to immerse my mind and thoughts in Yours, so that I stop speaking in a way that is dishonouring to who I truly am by grace. Transform my thoughts and help me to understand how marvellously made I am in You. Baptize my habits in Your knowledge of me. The old way of seeing myself or anyone else is over; help me use my tongue to speak beauty, hope and favour whenever I speak about anyone, including myself.

Amen.

Prayer for Alignment

Loving, Eternal and most gracious Father of my Lord Jesus, forgive me for the moments when I have underestimated Your Son, Jesus Christ. Forgive me for the times I have dishonoured Him and His place in this universe. Forgive me for believing more in Adam and his fall than in Your Son and His incarnate life, death, resurrection and ascension.

Awakening to the mystery of Christ in me is the point of the good news You always wanted me to understand. I celebrate Your love, kindness, and grace towards me before I was even formed in the womb of my blessed biological mother. Before anything was made, You had me in your community of love in eternity. I was associated in Christ before the fall of the world. Your beloved, faithful and eternal Son, Jesus Christ, is the manifestation of Your mind made up about me. He is all You see when You think about me. You always knew, in Your love for me, that You would present me again face-to-face before Yourself in Christ, in a blameless and irreproachable innocence. Thank You Father, In Christ.

Amen.

Prayer for Friends

Dear Abba Father, in the awareness of Your unending love for the human race, I freely want to talk to You about [**name of friend(s)**]. I thank You because You love [**name of friend(s)**] more than I do and You care about them as well. Father, I ask of You to open [**name of friend(s)**] eyes to see and realize that [**he/she**] has been graced with Your peace, joy, rest, courage, patience, kindness, gentleness, faithfulness, self-control and love. In whatever circumstance [**he/she**] may be in right now, I ask You, my Father in Heaven, to meet [**him/her**] in [**his/her**] need; and allow [**him/her**] to continuously open up to Your love, until they fall even deeper in love with You. Soak [**his/her**] heart and mind in your joy and let [**him/her**] melt before your beautiful face.

Give [**name of friend(s)**] dreams and visions to guide [**his/her**] direction and choices. Bless [**him/her**] with ideas that only come from You in order for [**him/her**] to walk right on the patterns You preordained for [**him/her**] in Christ Jesus.

May Your Spirit persuade [**name of friend(s)**] of the radiance of Jesus. Provoke [**him/her**] with divine hope and courage. Give [**him/her**] simplicity of heart towards anyone who could be part of [**his/her**] world or sphere of influence.

This I pray in the Name of Jesus Christ

Amen.

Prayer for Healing of the Soul

Father in heaven, in the freedom of Your endless love and in the safety of Your embrace, I admit that sometimes somethings happen to me and I get lost in the darkness. Instead of living in Your joy, I get crippled inside. Instead of receiving Your love, my soul is disturbed. I become needy. I shut down and withdraw, and I become self-centred, angry, and frustrated. In my pain, I find myself hurting those that I love. I waste time and life. I am so embarrassed that I am scared to look at myself. Forgive me, my Father, for blaming others for my problems.

Speak to my soul, Father. Tell me again that there is more to me than I know. Help me believe that my existence, my life, and my future is part of Yours. Help me to see that facing my life and my hurt means liberation and fullness, not death. Show me where, when, and how I am not receiving Your love for me. Show me how my fear is attached to people, places, events, smells, and things. Deliver me from the triggers and associations of evil. Forgive me for what I have said and done, and even for what I have not said and done to Your children. Dad, I belong to You. You commissioned Your Spirit to resonate the Abba echo in my heart and now, in my innermost being, I recognize You as my only true and very dear Father. In Christ I pray.

Amen.

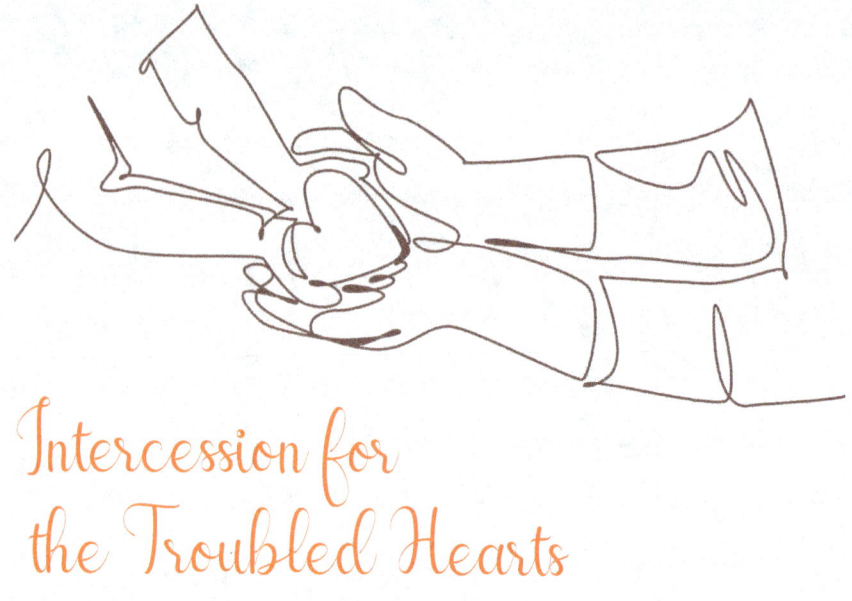

Intercession for the Troubled Hearts

Lord Jesus, You are close to the brokenhearted and You save those who are crushed in spirit. I ask that You bless the hungry souls who brave the seas of our illusions, to behold what we avoid seeing with all our hearts. What painful joy they feel on the lonely paths they walk. Give them Your light, courage, and steadfastness. Don't let them lose heart. Save them from fear. Save them from the crowd. Save them from the sneers of the religious types who embrace the dark in Your name. Give their spouses freedom to encourage. Fire them with the Spirit of adoption. Never let them lose hope on following their future dreams.

Thank You, Lord Jesus Christ, for doing it unto them, according to Your Word.

Amen.

Prayer of a Repentant and Grateful Heart

Precious Saviour, You are my salvation, rescuer, and redeemer. Jesus, Your heart is so true and passionate, that You refused to camp out on the frontiers of my darkness, and to watch me destroy myself from a distance. You crossed all worlds to enter into my world, in order to save me from darkness. Where it was impossible for me to see our Father, You recalibrated my ability to see Him through Your eyes. My love for You is sustained by Your love for me.

I am forever grateful because nothing *good or wrong* that I did or didn't do stopped You from sharing with me all that You are and have. I love You because of Your unwavering and irrepressible desire for me to see Your Father in You, to know Him as You know Him and to live in the joy of His embrace, as You do in the freedom of the Spirit. My spirit, soul and body belong to You forever.

Thank You, Jesus.

Amen.

Prayer from a Re-Acclimated Heart

Marvellous and precious Holy Spirit, to You belongs the power, might, wisdom, joy, and love. Without You there would be no union or fellowship with our Father in heaven, only separateness. Thank You for Your endless burden to bring the life of the Father and Son into expression in us.

Forgive me for not seeing so much of what You are doing in me, with me and through me. Help me to see how I am participating in Your work. Help me to see where I work against You. Do not be grieved at my blindness and hardness of heart. I am blind; please open my eyes to see who Jesus really is and what He shares with His Father. Help me break through my legalistic mindset and see reconciliation, as Jesus worked it out in His own experience. You are my faithful, merciful, and ever-present best companion. Adjust my sight, so that I partake even better in the life of my design. I love and value Your presence in and with me, for every millisecond of my life.

Thank You, dear Holy Spirit.

Amen.

Prayer to Counter Evil / Darkness

Eternal Father, Son, Holy Spirit, I belong to You. I want no part in darkness. I want to participate in Your relationship. Every form of evil and darkness that could possibly do me harm are silenced and bound. I give You permission to create space in my soul, to feel Your joy. From this place, I want to look at what is going wrong and see every bit of it bathed in Your grace and peace.

Any soul tie that I have that is not in Your will is silenced right now. Heal my soul, my mind, and thoughts from whatever is not Your will. Whatever is mine that I lost, I call it back to me. Preserve me from participating in any form of evil or darkness. Thank You for never abandoning me. Thank You, that You watch out for me in Your steadfast love. You are my Love and Lover, my Lord and God, my eternal and faithful Saviour, my Redeemer and Rescuer; my satisfaction, peace, healing, righteousness, wisdom, joy, comforter, companion and my Life.

God in your Holy Trinity, I worship You

Amen.

Prayer for Inner Rest

Precious and blessed Lord Jesus, You are the Lamb of God, the Redeemer and Rescuer of God's image and likeness in me. You became what I was, so that I can become what You are. I am in You and I am a partaker of all that You are and all that You have in Your relationship with your Father.

When You talk to me, I hear You speak my name, and with the freedom of Your heart, I turn towards the Father to see Him through Your eyes. I receive the witness of the Spirit of Adoption each time I behold the face of our Father in heaven, through Your eyes. I receive our Father's everlasting love, and I give myself, all of me, freely to our Father's embrace. I am baptized in the joy of the Holy Spirit. I am blessed and highly favoured in You.

Thank You, Jesus.

Amen.

Prayer Against Fear

Blessed Holy Spirit, You are omniscient (knowing everything), omnipresent (always everywhere), omnipotent (all powerful) and omni-sapient (all wise). I thank You for encircling and holding me safe and secure in Your joy. Jesus broke me free from captivity by dying in my place, and by His resurrection, He held me as a trophy in His triumphant procession.

You repossessed unto me what belonged to me by design. I confess, my mind is wrapped up with the truth. Jesus said that You will guide me into all truth. Thank You for silencing every unpleasant emotion of fear, caused by the belief that someone or something is dangerous, likely to cause pain or is a threat. I am free from the dominion of any sense of terror, fright, and panic, for my thoughts are baptized in what the Father knows about me. Steady my emotions, sustain my soul, and align my perception of people and things with Yours.

Almighty God, beneath Your wings filled with light, I have no fear. As I wade through truth, clean and bright, I have no fear. As I dwell in love, safe at night, I have no fear. As I soak in Your hope and eternity signs, I have no fear. I love You, Holy Spirit.

Amen.

Prayer When Sad and Depressed

Dear Lord Jesus Christ, beloved, eternal, and faithful Son of God, thank You for Your gentle mercy on me in my sadness. Based on my union with You, I confess that I am not afraid of anything. I confess by faith, that I am not sad or depressed. I originate from God and have already conquered the worldly religious systems, because You live in me and I in You. Your living presence in me is far beyond the futile mindset present in this world. Sadness and depression cannot co-exist with Your love because Your love expels fear and all its fruits *of sadness, depression, guilt, stress, and anxiety.*

Share with me continuously, Your own experiential knowledge of Your Father's heart, so that I may know Your confidence, passion, joy and peace. Help me indulge in the Holy Spirit's intoxication, that I may be of service to You in Your liberation of the human race. Because of You, Lord Jesus, I am free, safe and sound today.

Thank You, Jesus.

Amen.

Acknowledge Jesus as My All

Worthy are You, Lord Jesus Christ. You are the Father's beloved Son; the Anointed One, the Lamb of God who took away the sins of the world, and the One who baptizes in the Holy Spirit.

Victorious Warrior, worthy are You of all praise, adoration, and worship, now and forever. Thank You for being my Saviour, my Good Shepherd, my High Priest, my true and faithful Witness, my Alpha and Omega. You are everlasting, eternal, wonderful, excellent, and highly exalted. I rest in You, and await to experience the extremities of Your goodness and kindness towards me today.

Amen.

Prayer from a Worried Heart

Gracious Father in Heaven, You are kind and wonderful, lovely, and merciful. You are excellent in all Your ways. My Father, in the awareness of Your unending love for me in Christ Jesus, I want to thank You for blessing me with all that You considered to be Your best. I am still in awe, when I think about all that You accomplished in Christ, and what I have become by Your grace. Sometimes, I get carried away in my own definition of my experiences and I fall in the trap of worrying about so many things in my life.

The world is a beautiful place to be in when I look at it through the perception of Your heart, but sometimes my perception drifts into seeing it as a mess when I watch TV, listen to the radio stations and even engage in social media. Help me to continuously grow in an experiential knowledge of Jesus. I am equipped and empowered by Your Holy Spirit to live a happy and fulfilled life each day. I declare that You are my only Hope. Through Your Holy Spirit, I will always know that You are in charge of making everything work out for the good of all that are Yours in Christ Jesus.

Thank you, Father. In Jesus Name.

Amen.

Prayer When Feeling Inadequate

Dear Father, You are the Maker of heaven and earth, and of all things visible and invisible. Thank You for beautifully and wonderfully creating me. Thank You for giving me worth and value in Your eyes.

Help me live the life You intended me to live. Help me abide, instead of strive; living peacefully and joyfully as an heir to Your Kingdom and co-heir with Christ. I am forever grateful that You choose me for a life of greatness. I live a glorious and transcendent life because I discover each day who I am in Christ. I am part of the chosen generation, the royal priesthood. You rescued and redeemed the 'me' that You have always known. You ordained me to live a life of excellence and manifestation of the fruits of righteousness.

Thank You, Heavenly Father. In Jesus Name I pray.

Amen.

Gratitude in the Midst of Pain

Father, You are almighty, awesome and all-powerful. I am sorry for the way I complain about my circumstances. I am sorry for the bad attitude I have when things don't go my way. I am grateful for all that You said is mine in Your beloved Son, Jesus.

Worries and anxieties are not part of the nature You imparted in me, through Your Holy Spirit. Your presence has invaded everything that concerns and belongs to me. I am safe, secure, blessed and completed in Christ. Help me learn how to gaze on Jesus, even in the midst of the storm.

I know that Your plans for my life are amazing. Help my heart not to worry and my soul not to be lost in the prison of self-centeredness, for You are faithful and truthful, kind, and lovely, sweet and gentle.

I love You, Father. In Jesus Name.

Amen.

Prayer for God's Provision

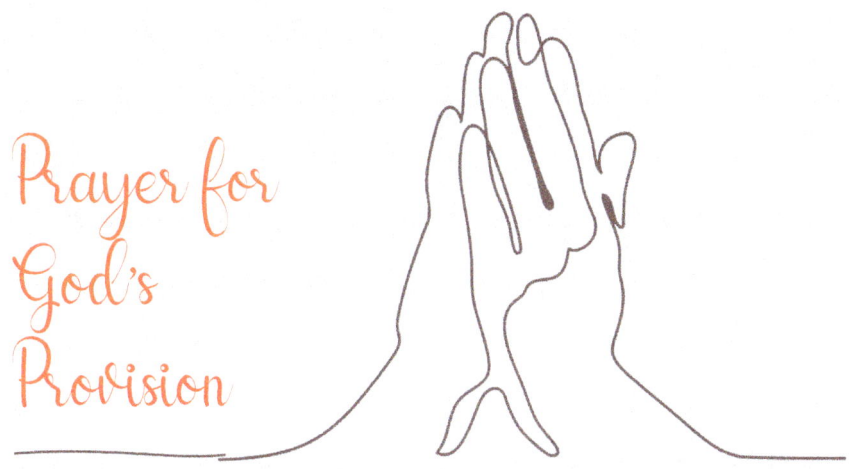

Dear Father in Heaven, You are beautiful and bountiful. You faithfully show Your generosity in my life every day. Thank You for Your unfailing love for me, Your blessings and unending goodness. Thank You for Your faithfulness that guides me and sees me through times of uncertainty, lifts me up, and sets me on high places. Thank You for Your Spirit that comforts me and reminds me of what You provided for me in Christ Jesus.

All my needs are met. I live under Your constant care and full supply. You provided for every single need I could possibly have, during every season of my life. Father, I thank You because whatever the provision for this season, time or day is, it manifests effortlessly in accordance to Your Word. Thank You for silencing every voice in me that suggests panic, fear, doubt, worry and all 'the what-ifs'. Remind me, through the gentle voice of Your Holy Spirit, that my help does not come from anyone or anything else, but from You. Grace me to be a good steward of everything that You give me to invest, sow and manage it wisely.

In Jesus Christ's Name.

Amen.

Participating in the Faith of Jesus

Everlasting King, eternal Son of the Father incarnate, excellent and exalted Lord, Jesus Christ; help me see and know better how to participate in Your faith. Help me realize my misunderstanding and lack of knowledge regarding the effectiveness of seeing what You know, and of living in the consciousness of who You are. Do not be grieved at my blindness and hardness of heart. Instead, flood my thoughts, my mind and my soul with Your light, until I am able see to the unlimited riches that our Father has already made available for those who belong to Him.

Free me from any legalistic mindset, so I can live in the freedom of Your own experience of the Father's satisfaction. Adjust the eyesight of my heart, so I live by Your faith, even in the midst of chaos. Give me the desire and ability to see You, fellowship with You, and give thanks to You in any season, circumstances, and time. Thank You for sharing Your faith with me. Your love in and through me sets faith in motion; I will therefore lack nothing.

I love You dearly.

Amen.

Prayer for Confidence

Dear Jesus, You are the gentle and good Shepherd. You are the great and glorious redeemer of my soul. I thank You for helping me to let go the fear of failure, rejection, death, [**add your own word**]. I know that the evil one uses fear and doubt to hold me back from living boldly the life of my design. Glorious Saviour, forgive me for trying to generate Your results with human performances and abilities.

By Your Spirit, soak my awareness/consciousness in Your confidence of Your Father's love. By virtue of my union with You, I experientially enjoy the Father's embrace today. Help me live with this bold confidence every single second of my earthly experience.

Lord, I will not compare myself to others around me. I will keep my eyes on You and live a life that proclaims Your excellence and nature.

Amen.

Prayer for a Heavy-Hearted

Lord Jesus Christ, I rest in You, Lover of my soul, Saviour, High priest, King, Liberator, the Author and Finisher of my faith. You have included me in all that You are and have, in Your face-to-face communion with your Father, and You baptized me in Your own anointing in the Holy Spirit.

In Your presence I quiet my soul and I gaze at You, Jesus. You are all I have, all I need, if I happen to need anything, all I could possibly want, if I happen to want something. You are all in me. I live, move, and have my being in You; my all. You are my everything.

Lord Jesus, I lay before You all that weighs heavily on my heart. Reveal the errors that are not part of my true nature in You, but that are in me and I am not aware of. In the power of Your Spirit, baptize all weaknesses, fears, anxieties, and insecurities that could be found in me.

Thank You, Lord Jesus, for Your unending love for me. From now on, my choices will honour You.

Amen.

Prayer for Hope and Trust

Father in Heaven, You are the all-creating One. Your love and belief about me are unchangeable, even though sometimes it feels as if You are not present in what I am going through. Sometimes I call and call again and it feels as if You cannot hear me when I need You the most. The distractions of my world succeeded in imprisoning my mind and my perception, instilling desires that are not of You. I do not want to keep living a life that is not designed for me.

I am beloved in Your Beloved Son. All I want right now is to feel Your divine embrace. Settle my heart in Your grace, until the smallest fragment of it is graced with grace, so that when I face a crisis in life [**my marriage, family, my education, ministry or career**], I will find joy and fulfilment in You alone. I know that You are with me. Submerge my mind with the confidence of Your love. The dynamics of my strategy is in Your ability to disengage my mindset and perception from what has held me captive. Christ is my victory. I am not a slave to anyone or anything. I trust You, Father, and even in the midst of contradiction I will trust You.

In the Name of Jesus Christ.

Amen.

Prayer for Contentment and Gratitude

O great Love, sometimes life gets me down and I find it hard to see things to be thankful for. Open my eyes to see the love that You unveiled within me in Christ Jesus. He was begotten of You in the flesh and sent into the world so that I might live. My life is mirrored and defined in Him. Both His birth in the flesh as well as His commission into the world was entirely Your doing. I thank You because Your love for me is not defined by my love for You.

I thank You, Father, that my responses to You don't qualify me to get Your attention. I have always had Your undivided affection, as it was declared by the prophets, and now demonstrated in Jesus, the faithful, beloved Son incarnate. Thank You, my Father, for giving me Your best as a gift. I am forever grateful, for there is nothing I can or could possibly need in this life, or the life to come, that can match the value of what You have given me in Christ.

In Jesus name.

Amen.

Heart To Heart Talk

❝

Let the Spirit Lead

Amen.

Prayer for Restoration in Relationships

Father God, open my eyes to see the mess in my soul and the damages I am causing around me. Help me to see the conflicts that I am allowing to brew in my family, my relationships, at my job, and in my own mind. Open my eyes to see the anger that is bubbling into murderous rage in my relationships.

Father, I thank You for showing me how hatred kills relationships. Instead of dwelling in what is wrong, I choose the way of love. Love is patient and kind, love is not jealous, it does not brag, and it is not proud. Love is not rude, it is not selfish, and cannot be made angry easily. Love does not remember wrongs done against it. Love is never happy when others do wrong, but it is always happy with the truth. Love never gives up on people, it never stops trusting, never loses hope and never quits. Everything will come to an end, but Love will not. Therefore, my Father, I ask You to invade my entire being (**my soul, mind, thoughts, conscience, sub-conscience**) with Love, so that I can love just like You love me.

Your way is always best, my Father. In Christ I pray.

Amen.

Awakening of Souls to the Knowledge of Jesus

Abba dear Father, You are the God and Father of our Lord Jesus, the Anointed One. You are the Father of glory. I call out to You on behalf of this generation. Your love for my brothers and sisters around the world is undeniable. I pray that You will help them with the struggles they are going through in their perception and in their soul. For You know exactly what they need in their blindness, pain, or darkness. Reveal to them how near to them You already are. Open their eyes, ears, and hearts to Your gospel, for the liberation of their perception of self into Yours. Disturb them with the fire of Your love, until they finally encounter Jesus in the darkness of their soul.

Abba Father, ignite in them the spirit of wisdom and revelation, in the unveiling of what You have known all along about them. Flood their hearts with inspired insights on the person and works of Your incarnate Son, Jesus Christ. Shine Your light on the hope that You are calling them to embrace. Reveal to them the glorious riches You have prepared as their inheritance. Let them see the full extent of Your power, that is at work in those who can see Jesus.

I pray in Christ.

Amen.

Prayer for a Suffering Friend

Eternal and immortal Father, You are loving, kind, attentive, tender and very caring. I forever thank You for Your love for [**name of your friend**]. It is so hard for me to watch [**him/her**] suffer this much. It doesn't seem fair for [**him/her**] to have to endure so much pain. Even though I am not able to change [**his/her**] situation, I believe You are right by [**his/her**] side. The powers of Your love and care for [**name of your friend**] interrupts every influence of darkness in [**his/her**] situation, and the outcome is completely and peacefully altered.

In the light of my participation in the faith, I thank You because in Christ Jesus, the detail of every single promise of God for [**his/her**] life is fulfilled. Your dear Son, Jesus, is Your answer to [**name of your friend**]'s entire well-being. In union with Him, the 'amen[that echoes in [**name of your friend**] gives evidence to Your glorious intent, in and through [**him/her**] and [**his/her**] life. I know You heard my prayer and You have already provided the way out for [**him/her**]. Therefore, my Father, I thank You because everything divinity touches is transformed and healed. [**His/her**] life is totally transformed by the power of Your resurrection.

I love You, gracious Father, loving and kind God. In Christ Jesus I pray.

Amen.

Prayer for Physical Healing

Loving Jesus, You are the Holy and Anointed One, the precious Redeemer and Saviour of the human race. Sickness is not from You, God. I believe in the victory purchases with Your death at the cross and Your resurrection, rather than the defeat from Adam's fall and all its consequences. I was once dead in the first Adam, thus, under the influence of all the consequences of the fall of God's creation. However, in You I have been made alive. Everything connected to the first Adam, and all the consequences of what He did wrong, died when You died in my place. I, therefore, have no connection with the old man, because my old self or mistaken identity was included in Your crucifixion, death, and burial.

I acknowledge that I co-raised, co-ascended and now I am co-seating at the Father's right hand with You. My old lifestyle was co-crucified together with You, and this concludes that the vehicle that accommodates sin, sickness, disease, pain or anything that does not reflect completeness and wholeness in me, was scrapped and rendered entirely useless, ineffective, outdated, silenced and unable to destroy or diminish the quality of life in my body. Sickness cannot have dominion over me anymore, for I am a brand-new person in God. I am alive, free, whole and in perfect health.

Thank You, Lover of my soul.

Amen.

Prayer for a Life Partner

Dear and all-knowing Father, I have been **single for several years** now, looking for a companion and life **partner with whom to** embark in the beautiful journey of "others-centred" love. I know You did not intend for me to live alone. Father, allow me to find a genuine lover of Jesus with whom to share love, dreams, joy, pain and life. I entirely depend on You, Father, to keep me from trying to satisfy my own desires by looking at everyone as a potential husband/wife. You love me and You have taken care of every detail of my life. My deepest thoughts and emotions will continuously be immersed in Your love.

Thank You for igniting the spirit of discernment and perception in me, in order for me to know what I need and what I do not need. I thank You because You will lead me to be with the person I need, not someone I simply want. I want to keep growing in the knowledge of Your Son, Jesus Christ, so I ask You to protect my heart and mind. Silence every thought or voice of self-centeredness, along with all its fruits that could be found in me. You know me better than I know myself, so I am open to see the love You placed within, my heart being directed towards the one You trust. I am tired of being alone and manipulated. I have so much love in my heart to share and give. Please hear my prayer.

Thank you, Father. In Christ I pray.

Amen.

Prayer for Someone's Awakening

Sovereign, Omniscient and Omnipresent Lord, You loved me and allowed me to see You in me. At the beginning You spoke into nothingness and brought forth heaven and earth. All creation responds to Your voice: The winds move, and the mountains shake at Your command; the stars, moon and sun are held by the power of Your will.

I believe You are the Creator, the Ruler of all. Everything exists in and for Your purpose. I want to thank You for the life of [**name of the person**]. Please open [**his/her**] eyes Lord, that [**he/she**] may see Your wide-open arms for them, just like the father of the prodigal son. He never thought anything different of his son. He embraced him and received him. Instead of being focused on what his son did wrong, he saw an opportunity of romance with his son again. His dead son was alive again, the one who was lost was finally found.

Father, I know that this parable reflects Your love for us. May this be the testimony of [**name of the person**]. Meet [**him/her**] in [**his/her**] darkness, weakness, brokenness, loses and despair. Disturb [**name of the person**] until [**he/she**] encounters Your irresistible love. I know You love [**him/her**] and You will never stop manifesting Your blessing throughout [**his/her**] life.

In Christ.

Amen.

Prayer for Strength

Dear Abba Father, I hear You speak my name, and with the freedom of my heart in Christ, I turn towards You to see Your face through Jesus' eyes. I acknowledge that You have always been in me, with me and for me. You gave me Your Holy Spirit, so that when I do not know how to pray; He can intercede for me. I am experiencing a challenging period right now. God, I do not understand why everything around me looks so dark and hopeless; weakness, helplessness and fear are settling in slowly. Even in this crisis, help my eyes and heart to stop turning away from You and to stop searching for help in what is perishable or temporary. Let Your Holy Spirit remind my heart of Your love for me. Just like Paul says: "*Everything works for the good of those who love you.*"

I thank You because Your love for me is causing everything to mutually contribute to my advantage. Because You care about me, this situation will turn to be a great testimony. I thank You for baptizing my weakness with Your joy, which is my strength. Your joy takes over my heart and carries me, so that I am able to endure this situation and be able to handle it in a way that will glorify Your name.

I give myself in love to You; all of me, to Your embrace, and to the healing of the Holy Spirit's life inside of me, that I may walk in every way, in the glorious freedom of the children of God.

In Christ.

Amen.

Prayer for Employment in Trying Times

Dear Lord Jesus, You are the Way, Truth and Life to me. It is written: *"When you open a door, no one can shut it; and when you shut it, no one can open."* I believe You care about me and want me to prosper in every sector of life. Everything good comes from You, including every perfect gift. These good gifts come down from Your Father, who made all the lights in the sky. You never change like the shadows from those lights.

You are always the same and I thank You for Your Holy Spirit within me. Your Spirit guides me on the search for a new job. You already know all things and know where I will be working. I need **(amount)** per hour/month/year and **(be specific)** as the benefits. Thank You for igniting the map of the way I am supposed to follow in my heart. In the enjoyment of Your peace, I thank You for the right position at the right job at the right time.

With the assistance of Your Spirit, I will not let discouragement set in. No matter the ups and downs, I will rejoice in You, Jesus.

Amen.

Prayer for a Friend Who is Moving

Blessed Lord Jesus Christ, I want to appreciate the presence of Your Spirit in and with my friend right now. I thank You because I know that You are more concerned about [**him/her**] than I am. I want to thank You because I believe You will help [**him/her**] as [**he/she**] gets settled in [**his/her**] new world (New city/ town/ State/ Country). Direct [**him/her**] during settlement into a new job and home. Bless [**him/her**] with genuine friends that will guide [**him/her**] to learn about the city, town and about where things are located to make [**his/her**] transition easier.

Dip any nervousness or anxiety into Your unearthly peace and joy. Through Your Spirit, preserve [**his/her**] heart in the confidence of Your Father's love. By virtue of Your oneness with [**him/her**], [**he/she**] will consistently enjoy Your Father's care and embrace throughout [**his/her**] journey from this day forward.

Amen.

Prayer for Inner Stillness

Heavenly Father, my instinct is to rush in and make plans, especially if someone I care about has made mistakes. Lord, remind me of the chalk line around my feet. Disturb my thoughts with Your love when I start thinking outside what You think and believe about me. Grace me with the ability to trust You in any circumstance, and to allow Your work in my soul, mind and body to be perfected as it is in Your dear Son, Jesus. As He is, so am I right now, in this world. Nothing that is in Him is missing within me, and whatever is not in Him and cannot touch or influence Him; should equally not be in me, touch or influence me. I trust You, Father, no matter what.

Forgive my ignorance. I have allowed strange voices to suggest to me [**mind and thoughts**] realities that pertain to a mistaken identity, and I have allowed my body [**Your temple**] to experience that which is not part of Your life in me (**sickness, weakness**). I ask You to please invade my soul with Your light, until the darkness is dissolved. Seize my mind with Your love, until the awareness of what I am in You becomes the song I sing, even when I am asleep. Through Jesus, allow me to experience Your divine embrace all the days of my journey on earth with You. It is in your beloved Son Jesus Christ that I pray.

Amen.

Fellowship with Holy Spirit Regarding Ministry

Dear Holy Spirit, You are my Comforter, Best Friend, Partner and Confidant. I am thankful because through Your power, I was birthed into the family of God, with Christ as my one and only nature. You make it effortless and easier for me to realize how, in Christ, I am delivered and disconnected; soul, mind and thought, from the fall of the world and its effects. I am saved by the life of Christ, and His life secures me from any lie that could come from the tree of the knowledge of good and evil to distract me from beholding Jesus as He really is and be transformed into His image.

Thank You, precious Holy Spirit. You keep me away from whatever could be a distraction to capture my mind and thoughts. You gave me the full rights and privileges of sonship. I take part, by grace, in the fellowship of the Father and the Son. Ignite the authority I have been given in Christ. I thank You because the miracle working power is exhibited through me in this world, in everything I do and everywhere I go.

I am an ambassador of Christ in my generation, announcing the ministry of reconciliation: That God was in Christ when He reconciled the total cosmos to Himself. I am a manifestation of Christ in my world, as Christ said, *"He who has seen me, has seen the Father…"* I can boldly say; anyone who sees me, sees Christ in an experiential way, through my flesh. I am a son in the Son of God, for I am sealed with You, and Your mark in me cannot be erased by anyone or anything.

Amen.

Thanksgiving for Being Blessed

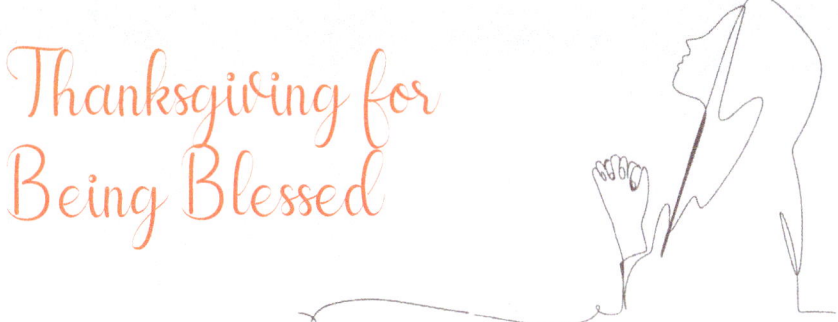

Dear Lover of our souls, Redeemer, Saviour, Righteous and Anointed One in the Holy Spirit. Jesus, I thank You for Your great love and blessings over my life. Thank You that Your favour has no end, but it lasts forever. You are intimately acquainted with all of my ways. You know what concerns me, even before I think about a thing, and I am covered as with a shield. I ask for Your guidance, so that I might walk fully in the blessings and goodness You already made available for me.

Today, I agree with what You made me to become in You. I am blessed with every blessing heaven could possibly have. There is absolutely no thought or idea of curse that could possibly affect or work against me, because I am not the one living now, it is Christ living in me, as me and through me. If I still live in my body, I live your faith in me. You are the One who loved me and shared your life with me. There is absolutely no trace of the fall of Adam and its influence that can be found in me, because I am dead to the old me that I was trying to be, and I am now alive to the real me, which is Christ in me. I was in You, in Your death, now I discover that You are infused in me, in my life.

Today, I confess that I am free to be me in my skin, immersed in Your faith, in our joint sonship. You love me and believe in me. You are the Father's gift to me, with me and in me. I love you.

Amen.

Prayer for Wisdom

Heavenly Father, I worship You and acknowledge Your strength and wisdom throughout all ages. Father, You are the God and Father of my Lord and Saviour Jesus the Christ. I feel the battle in my soul, and I am unable to handle it on my own. It is beyond the point of my sanity, but I make my request to You because I realize that I lack wisdom and it has cost me pain and loses. Fear and doubt are at the gate of my thoughts.

I believe that You are the origin and author of wisdom. I ask of You to intertwine my thoughts with Your good judgment. Whenever I am about to decide, let Your wisdom ignite from within and influence my heart and perception, so that my choices and decisions mirror Your pre-ordained plans in my life. I appreciate the fact that You will always be there for me, with me and in me. I will never be alone, ever. Even when I am in the darkest routes or walking through the fire; You are and will always be there. Thank you, Dad, for Your love and faithfulness towards me, in Christ Jesus

Amen.

Prayer for Identity

Lord Jesus, beloved brother, eternal saviour, and faithful Son of the Father incarnate. I am so grateful that You shared Your knowledge of Your Father's heart with me. My heart is filled with thanksgiving because I live, move, and have my being in You – You live and move in me as well. I stand in Your victory over death, fear, sickness, and anything that does not belong in Your nature and character. I am the righteousness of God because of you and I have been reconciled to God, once and for all. I have been perfected and sanctified in You forever.

I am so grateful because the Father loves me beyond my human comprehension. Everything that belongs to You as the beloved Son incarnate of the Father, is equally mine by grace. I partake into all that You shared with me; Your relationship with Your Father, life, authority, anointing in the Holy Spirit, peace, joy, Kingship and Lordship. You have made me an heir of this world, the planet, its systems, and resources. My words cannot explain or define the greatness of what You did for me and with me, and what You continuously do in me and through me in our journey together. Thank You.

Amen.

Heart To Heart Talk

❝

Let the Spirit Lead

Amen.

Declaration of Belonging

Beloved, eternal, and faithful Son of the Father, Jesus, You are the crucified, resurrected, and ascended Lord of all who sits at the right hand of the Father. You are above all rule and authority. While I marvel in front of Your greatness, I acknowledge every benefit, advantage, and good thing which is in me, because it is in You. In light of Your crucifixion, death, burial, resurrection, ascension, and seating at the right hand of the Father, I can freely and confidently say I am a member of the heavenly family. With Christ as my one and only nature, I am constantly (daily) delivered from the effects of death.

Precious Saviour, You live in me and Your life in me manifests itself in and through me, with irrefutable evidence in my whole spirit; soul, body and everything pertaining to my world. I ask Your Spirit to ignite the desire in my whole being, to consistently participate in every facet of Your life, and in the powers that are at work in me.

Amen.

Affirmation of My Position in Christ

Dear Father in Heaven, You are the Lover and Maker of heaven and earth. Today I come in agreement with You regarding Your thoughts concerning me, and I refuse to live my life like everyone else around me. I refuse to live my life as an ordinary person. Even though I live in this flesh, I am not just a mere person; I am a spirit being, and You are my origin.

Father, I thank You for helping me to be conscious of that reality today; conscious of You. I refuse to limit my joy in life to whatever is temporary. Nothing in this world has what it takes to satisfy me and produce Your Joy in me. I refuse to live for anything else but love. Abba Father, I acknowledge what is temporary and I set my eyes on what is eternal. Life (Jesus) is more than goals, notoriety, wealth, and the abundance of things a person can possess. Life is more valuable than Gold and Diamond, therefore, Father, I joyfully live daily in the fullness of the joy that is found in Your presence; in Your most immediate nearness. Father, I thank You, for the very romance of the ages we have been invited into; Your abundant life. At Your right hand there is fullness of joy and pleasures forevermore. In Christ I pray.

Amen.

Confession of the Measure of Christ

Eternal and immortal Father, thank You because my life cannot be measured by anything that I have or do not have, but by the grace that was given to me according to the measure of Jesus Christ.

Dear Father, I praise You for blessing me with an inheritance in Christ that cannot be measured, taken, or destroyed. In the consciousness of this enlightenment, I declare that goodness and mercy are indeed following me and running in me from everywhere, all the days of my life. Oh, how wonderful it is to dwell secure in the heart of my Father forever and ever! Surely, I have finally found The Life (Jesus Christ), when I lost my life. I rest hidden and secure in Christ in God. You are the Alpha and Omega; You alone are my life and the fullness of my joy.

Christ is indeed my all in everything. Surely, Your life and joy preserved and sealed me in Your Spirit. Neither time nor disaster can diminish or take away what I have and enjoy in You. No temporal circumstance has what it takes to limit my approach before You. Because of Your mercy, my limited mortal ability cannot disqualify me from the enjoyment of the fullness of Your nearness. I pray as a son in your Son

Amen.

Confession of Spiritual Awakening

Beautiful and loving Father, I am very grateful that You know me inside-out, better than anyone, including myself. You free me thoroughly from any hidden alliance with the old system of performance-based living. There is absolutely no temporary circumstance that can change my worth in Christ. I am eternally grateful to You, my Lord and Lover of my soul, that You came to seek and save the lost. Thank You so much for what You have brought me into: eternal joy, inexhaustible blessing, and fullness of glory. Your thoughts of our oneness inspire me. I cannot help but continue to celebrate your life in me. Thank You, Father God, for awakening your Spirit's reality within my spirit. Your Spirit reality is indeed a greater reality than the mortal reality we live our lives in, and far surpasses it in glory. In Christ.

Amen.

Intercession for Healing Our World

Oh great Love, awesome God, thank You for living in us and loving through us. May all that we do flow from our deep connection with You and all beings.

Help us become a community that vulnerably shares each other's burdens and the weight of glory. Listen to our hearts longings for the healing of our world. [**Please state your own heart's longings for the world**]. Knowing You are hearing me better than I am speaking, I offer this prayer in the holy name of Jesus Christ.

Amen.

Prayer for Intimacy

Lord Jesus, I give the whole of my being and yield into the intimacy of knowing and being known. Help me be completely vulnerable and self-giving in the process of seeking intimacy.

Divine Lover, You are absolutely real and for those willing to bear the wounds of intimacy, the knowledge of that underlying coherence — 'in which all things hold together' — is both possible and inevitable.

Thank You, dear Lord Jesus.

Amen.

Thanksgiving for Restoration

Gracious, loving and merciful Father, I thank You for the work of Christ Jesus upon the cross on my behalf.

I acknowledge that You did it all in Him so that I may receive it all from a state of rest, not struggle. I acknowledge that Christ is my life. From Him flows healing, restoration, freedom, righteousness, wholeness, prosperity, holiness, perfection, joy, peace, and favor. As a partaker, my part is to partake.

All things are mine in Christ. Thank You, Abba Father. In Jesus Christ I pray.

Amen.

Acknowledging Jesus Christ

Abba Father, Thank You for the substitution of Jesus Christ. He was made a curse in my place.

On the cross, He took all that was associated to Adam and his fall. When He died, Adam's fall was buried once and for all. My curses were buried; sicknesses were buried; poverty was buried; and death was buried.

I acknowledge and agree today that Jesus Christ has always been Lord, even over my life. From now, I ask of His Spirit to teach me how to live by His faith. I belong to God, I am blessed beyond my imagination, I am whole, prosperous and rich; preserved, complete, entire and I definitely have all things. In Christ I pray.

Amen.

Prayer of Gratitude for Insight

Eternal Father, I thank You because You continually give me the Spirit of wisdom and revelation, the spirit of hearing and seeing, and I am inspired with true insight into Your mysteries and secrets.

I am continuously growing in the fuller, deep and intimate knowledge of Christ. The eyes of my understanding are flooded with light and my heart is continuously in an enlightened state. My mind is open to see and perceive. I am experiencing inner illumination of the spirit.

Today, Father, I know You in a more comprehensive manner, beholding the ever-increasing view of the hope of Your calling for me in Christ. Thank You, my Father. In Christ Jesus I pray.

Amen.

Prayer to Start the Day

Oh, dear Love, our Father, and our God, at the start of this day, help me to recognize You above all else. Enlighten the eyes of my heart that I may see You and notice how You are at work through my life.

Give me wisdom to make the best choices. Supply my heart with the desire to walk in the paths You ordained for me to walk in today. May Your Spirit breathe upon me and whatever I am around today. Your fragrance reaches and beautifies everything I touch today. Thank You that You are greater than anything I may face in my day.

Thank You that Your presence always goes with me, and that Your joy is never dependent on my circumstances, but it is my true and lasting strength, no matter what I am up against. Your peace leads me and guards my heart and mind in Christ. I celebrate the virtues of Your grace on me and with me today. My life is hidden in You today: Untouchable and unstoppable. I love You, great Love. In Christ I pray.

Amen.

Prayer from a Heavy Heart

Hello Father, I am very thankful to be graced in You. My heart is heavy, I feel like I have to carry the burden alone [**share the burden with Him**]. Words like overwhelmed, distraught, exhausted seem to describe where I am right now. I am not sure how to let You carry my heavy load, so please show me how. Take it from me.

Let me rest and be refreshed so that my heart will not be so heavy in the morning. In the holy name of Jesus.

Amen.

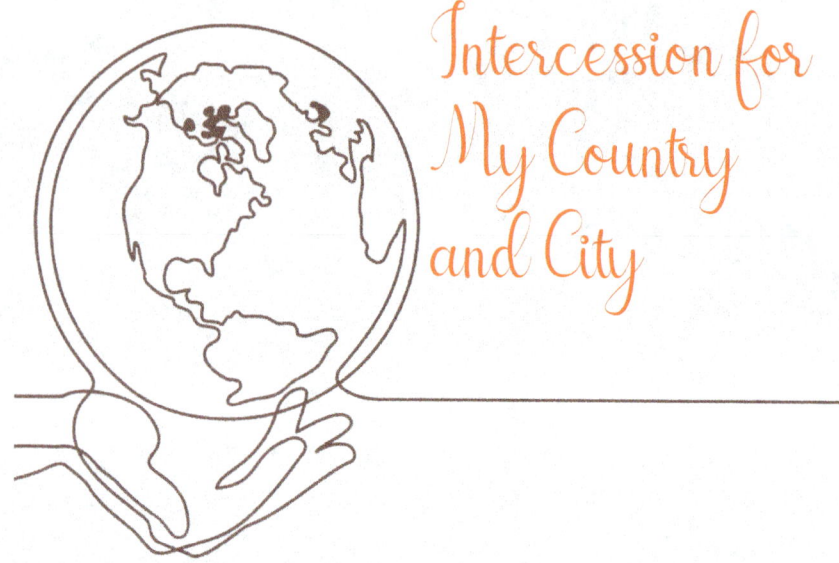

Intercession for My Country and City

My dear loving God, you have set us together into families and clans; into countries, cities and neighbourhoods. Our common life began in a garden, but our destiny lies in the city. You have placed us in [**city or country**]. This is our home. Your creativity is on display here in [**city or country**] through the work of human hearts and hands. We pray for [**city or Country**] today – for the East Side, West Side, North and South.

We pray for our poorest cities, neighbours and for our governments; we pray for people of power and authority in the country, institutions, and offices downtown. We pray for people from the 'hood', the barrio and for the new urbanites in our city, and a thousand other cities connected to our own. In all our neighbourhoods, this day, there will be crime and callous money-making. There will be powerful people unable or unwilling to see the vulnerable who are their neighbours.

There also will be beautiful acts of compassion and creativity in all these places; forgiveness and generosity and neighbours working together for a more just community.

Dear Father in Heaven, please help us to see this place as something other than a battleground between us and them; where our imaginations are limited by win/lose propositions and endless rivalry. Show us a deeper reality, dear God. Show us your playground and invite us to play. Like the city of your dreams, make this a **country/ city** where those who were once poor enjoy the fruits of their labour. Make it a place where children are no longer doomed to misfortune but play safely in the streets under the watchful eyes of healthy old men and women. Transform it into a place where former rivalries and natural enemies work and play together in peace; where all people enjoy communion with you. We pray in the Name of the One who wept over our city; our Lord Jesus Christ.

Amen.

Prayer to Manifest Sonship

Precious Jesus, You are the light of my world. I am grateful to You that You made me an instrument of Your peace.

> Where there is hatred, let me sow love;
> Where there is injury, let me sow pardon;
> Where there is doubt, let me sow faith;
> Where there is despair, let me sow hope;
> Where there is darkness, let me sow light;
> Where there is sadness, let me sow joy.

Grant that I may not so much seek to be consoled as to console; to be understood as to understand; to be loved as to love. For it is in giving that I receive. Because I was pardoned, I will pardon, and it is because I died in Your death that I am born to eternal life.

Thank you, Jesus.

Amen.

Heart To Heart Talk

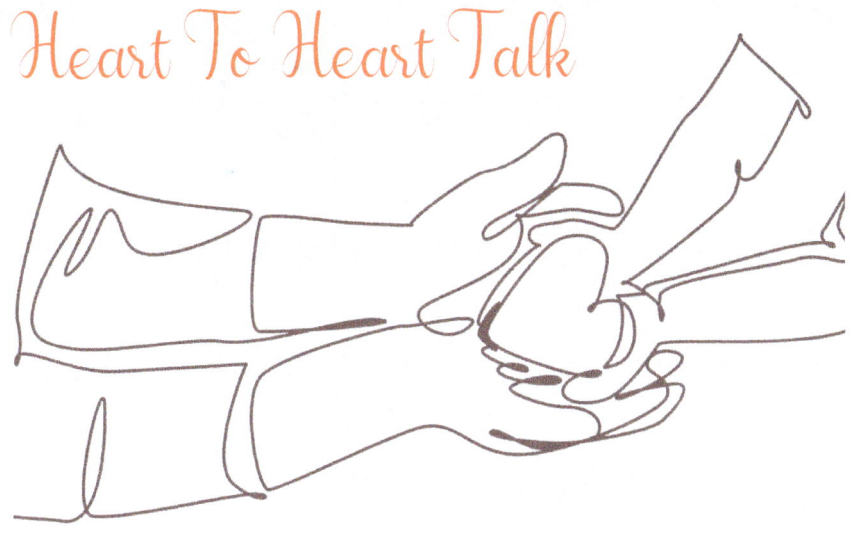

"
Let the Spirit inspire you

Amen.

Heart To Heart Talk

"

Let the Spirit guide you

_____
_____
_____
_____
_____
_____
_____
_____
_____
_____
_____
_____

Amen.

Heart To Heart Talk

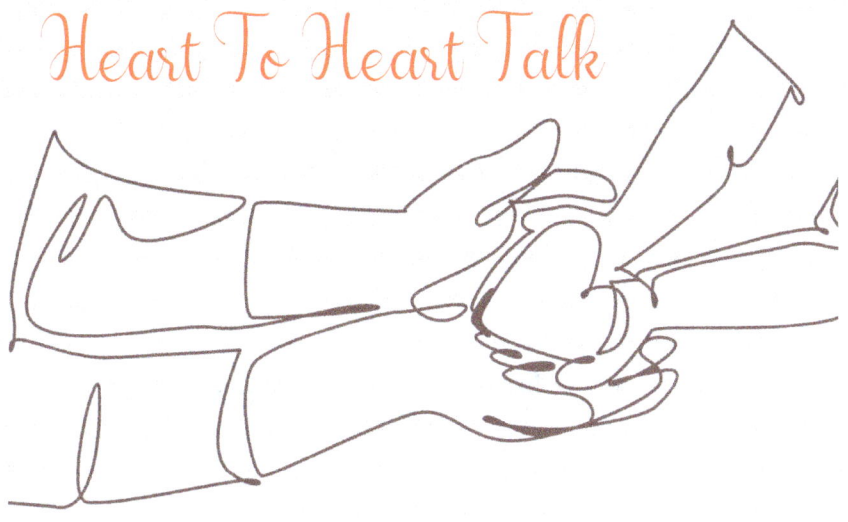

> Speak your heart out

_____

_____

_____

_____

_____

_____

_____

_____

_____

Amen.

IMPORTANT

In the early church, Christians were deeply committed to Jesus' teachings. They lived faithfully by them. Their chosen solitude and silence were not anti-social, but a way to become better at seeing clearly and at loving deeply. Withdrawal was for the sake of deeper encounter and presence.

Speaking of the relationship between contemplation and action, there is a natural flow from solitude to prayer to active love. For those who went to the desert,

> *Come follow me...*
>
> **[MATTHEW 19:21]**

it was not an escape from their daily lives but rather it served as an alternative practice of engagement; the first step on the way towards becoming a new people, a universal community of God's love.

Their response to Jesus' call, "*Come follow me*", was intimately bound up with the practice of prayer. Prayer connects us with God and with others. Prayer is much more than a technique; it is a disposition of wholeness. Prayer must be a part of our daily lives.

We should approach prayer as the early church Christians, as a practical two-fold process: First, '**of thinking and reflecting**' or '**pondering**' what it means to love others; and second, '**as the development and practice**

of loving ways of being'. In other words, prayer is participation in God's love, the activity that takes us out of ourselves, away from the familiar, and conforms us to the path of Christ.

We need to preach more through our lifestyles than through sermons. There were few 'doctrines' to prove that outer life is only changed from inward experience. To live without speaking, is better than to speak without living. The former who lives rightly, does good even by his silence, but the latter does no good even when he speaks. When words and life correspond to one another, they are together the whole of philosophy.

This dance of infinite love is rhythmically playing itself out in the rhythms of our life, standing up and sitting down, waking up and falling asleep. The rhythms of day by day, are the rhythms of love given to us, as this is the inherent sacred nature of life itself. Just as so many of the mystics have taught, doing what you are doing with care, presence, and intention is a form of prayer; the very way to transformation and wholeness. There is no trick or magic formula to becoming one with Reality. There is only living, and as you know, this is much harder than it first seems.

My Prayer for You

Most gracious and loving Father, You are not a slot machine that we can manipulate with our prayers, praise or pleas or even our personal sacrifices, if we just try long or hard enough to overcome Your reluctance to 'bless' us. You have already blessed us with every blessing heaven can possibly have. Disturb the thoughts, hearts, minds and souls of Your son/daughter who, because of blindness, distanced himself/herself mentally from You by believing lies about who he/she is and who You really are.

Your beloved and faithful Son, Jesus Christ, does not come to negotiate with You to bless us, if we jump through all the hoops. He is Your mind made up about [**your name**]. Jesus mirrors You in us and us in You, Abba Father. [**Your name**] is not defined by abuse or abundance. Whatever circumstances, challenges, difficulties, or even joyful moments come, You remain unchanged. Your Word regarding us remains true, whether we are facing a feast or a fast, a fountain or famine. Abundance is not a sign of Your goodness, our Father, neither is lack a sign of Your absence.

I declare and prophecy that in every situation of [**your name**]'s present life, [**he/she**] is strong in the One who empowers [**him/her**] from within to be who [**he/she**] has always been in the heart of God, our Father.

In Christ.

Amen.

From God

I, Your Ever present Father, declares according to My Word, that whatever You have lost in Your life (every earthly thing: Materials, relationships or opportunities that was once yours), My grace has brought it back to You.

This is Your season of grace experiences. Get ready for the manifestation of what I have made ready for you in My dear Son, Jesus Christ, before you were formed in your mother's womb. You are eternally blessed (See Genesis 12:3 – AMP).

Love,
Your Father in heaven

CONCLUSION

These prayers are neither the only way to pray nor are you wrong if you do not pray this way. This book has been about enlightening your heart to see what God sees and speak what His Love says, and what He believes about you. This is a heart to heart kind of conversation. I have prayed the wrong way too, and yet I still loved God and He loved me in my ignorance. But since I have been praying the way I have shared in this book, I have seen great improvements in the results I get. I just needed to stop worrying and start seeing what is already mine.

My prayer for you is that the Lord will take these words and prayers that I have shared with you, and bring you into a new understanding and deeper experience of what prayer is, so you can get results. I believe Love will use its own language to bring you out of any religious traditions that make your prayers of no effect. You will experience the freedom and joy that comes from having a heart to heart conversation with Papa.

As you experientially receive what is yours in Christ, I pray that Jesus will grant you opportunities to share this book with others so they too can begin to experience a different kind of conversation with Papa, Jesus, and Holy Spirit.

THE ULTIMATE INVITATION

Pray this prayer:

"Dear Father, in the freedom of Your endless love and in the safety of Your divine embrace, I acknowledge that Jesus Christ is Your eternal Son. I got lost in my own darkness, instead of living in Your joy. I got crippled inside, instead of receiving Your love; my soul was disturbed.

Today, I acknowledge and believe that the life of Jesus from His birth to His seating at the right hand of God was vicarious. I was co-crucified with Jesus; I co-died on the cross with Him; I was co-buried together with Him; on the third day I co-raised from among the dead with Him; I co-ascended on high with Jesus and I am co-seated at Your right hand with Him. I acknowledge in my heart and agree to the fact that Jesus Christ is Lord of all and overall.

I give myself in love to You today, just as You gave Yourself in love for me and to me. Here I am Father, Jesus, and Holy Spirit, LOVE me. Amen."

If you sincerely repeated these words, welcome back to your real senses.

The Father God welcomes you and celebrates your return [**return to the consciousness of your true identity**]. You are a partaker of the saving work and life of Jesus Christ. The journey of love and discovery has started.

It is important for you to continuously grow in the knowledge of the love, the person and finished work of Jesus Christ by allowing your soul to be fed with the words of grace. For you have been crucified with Christ, it is no longer you who live, but Christ lives in you. Therefore, the terms co-crucified and alive together with Christ defines you now. Christ in you and you in Him. It is a blessing to know that the life you live is entirely by the faith of another (Jesus Christ), so you have nothing to worry about from now on. He got your back from start to finish. Live your life overwhelmed by God's opinion of you.

I advise you to find a Christo-centric local church to learn more about Jesus, His Father and Holy Spirit, then you will discover who you really are and what already belongs to you by virtue of your origin and identity. Celebrate who you already are in God's family every single day of your life.

You matter to God!

I invite you to share with us the wonderful things God did in your life while fellowshipping with Him using this book. We would love to hear your reviews and feedback. You can also purchase additional copies of Heart to Heart to give away to those you care about.

For more information about booking the author to speak to your organization or group, please contact Christ In All Nations Inc at info@christinallnations.org.

If you enjoyed this book, here are some ideas to help you share this book with others:

» Give the book to friends, even strangers, as a gift. They are not just getting a compelling, page-turner, but also a magnificent glimpse into the true nature of God that is not often presented in cultures around the globe today.

» If you have a website or blog, consider sharing a bit about the book and how it touched your life. Do not give away the plot but recommend that they read it as well.

» Write a book review for your local paper, favourite magazine or website you frequent. Ask your favourite radio show or podcast to have the author on as a guest. Media people often give more consideration to the requests of their listeners than the press releases of publicists.

» If you own a shop, business or you are pastoring a church, consider putting a display of these books on your counter to resell to customers. We make books available at a discounted rate for resale. For individuals, we offer volume discount pricing for orders of five books or more.

» Buy a set of books as gifts to battered women's shelters, prisons, rehabilitation homes, and the like where people might be really encouraged by these prayers.

» Talk about the book on e-mail lists you are on, forums you frequent, and other places you engage other people on the internet. Share how this book impacted your life and offer people the link to the amazon book page.

For more information about Alain Lea, please visit:
www.christinallnations.org

ABOUT THE AUTHOR

For more than a decade, Alain Lea has been criss-crossing the world, spreading the Truth of the Gospel. His profound revelation is known for its clarity even while it retains the original simplicity of the Trinitarian Gospel. As the Director of Christ in All Nations, Apostle Lea has trained several ministers of the Gospel, in the United States of America and around the globe. His students are spread across America and different parts of the world, taking the good word of the Lord to millions of people yearning for the revelation of the sons of God.

A prolific author, Alain Lea has written numerous books, including "Freedom From Fears" and "Heart To Heart". His mastery over the Gospel, coupled with his understanding of the physical and emotional aspects of sufferings, have led him to pen books on diverse subjects. During the course of his long years in the service to the Lord and mankind, Alain Lea has produced an extensive collection of teaching materials – in print, audio, and video formats. His ministry is actively distributing free audio tapes and CDs to all the needy people who yearn for God's Love. Alain Lea can be contacted at:

dralainlea@christinallnations.org

or write to:

Christ In All Nations, Inc
P.O Box: 588
Granger, IN 46530

AVAILABLE ON AMAZON

The Void

"THE VOID is one of the most challenging and absorbing work of fiction I've read in many years. I laughed, prayed, cried; It is simply mind blowing and challenging at the same time. THE VOID will leave you craving for a better understanding of who God really is."

~ Apostle Ankur Narula, Church of Sighs and Wonders

In a world were religion seems to grow increasingly irrelevant, THE VOID wrestles with the timeless question: Where is God when He is needed the most? The answers will astound you and perhaps transform you. You will want everyone you know to read this book!

Christian was the only son his parents had, but both died before he had the chance to know them. He grew up with friends who became part of his life for many years. They all had very tragic stories to tell and were all experiencing a Void within that none of them could explain. After years of trying different things and ways to live a better life, they always ended up in more pain and trouble than before. In the midst of their greatest confusion, something very mysterious happened to one of them and left the others extremely suspicious. Apparently, God opened the eyes of Christian to the source of fulfilment. His life was gradually a reflection of pure beauty, with vision and purpose.

Now he is tasked with the mandate to reach his eight closest friends who have not known the freedom of living without the Void. They are in danger of being consumed and destroyed. He knows his window of opportunity is small because he has a vision of one of his friends dying, but he doesn't know which one.

What Now?

Once Lost Now Saved

It is so easy to forget what faith is all about. We struggle so much, work so hard, and fail so often that we frequently sense something in the equation of life must be missing.

Alain Lea argues that what we are missing is the gospel in a fuller, more powerful understanding of Jesus and what His finished work means for everyday life.

During his adolescence, Alain Lea discovered the power of the gospel in his own life by experiencing encounters with Jesus. He shares in this book what He learned when Jesus became more real to him. Lea delves deeply into the fundamentals of faith, explaining the implications of Christ's sufficiency as the revelation that sets us free and keeps us anchored through life's storms.

Ultimately, Alain reminds us that Jesus is the whole of the equation as he boldly proclaims that humanity was once lost and now found in Christ Jesus.

Freedom From Fears

'Freedom from Fears' by Apostle Alain Lea is a classic work that takes the reader on a journey of healing – physical as well as spiritual. In this book, the author who's a renowned preacher of more than two decades standing, in his element, methodically breaks down the anatomy of fear. Once he breaks down this scary emotion called FEAR, Apostle Lea then takes the readers on an exploratory journey of the realms of fear that we as normal human beings face in our daily lives. The book is systematically designed for effective reading – every chapter ends with key takeaways – so you know where to turn to when you're looking for a solution to your fears. The author has skillfully merged the physical and spiritual aspects of fear and its remedies. It's a handy book for readers of all age groups, whichever country you belong to, whatever your belief systems may be. 'Freedom from Fears' finally gives you the answers you were searching for in your quest for a fearless life!

BOOKS COMING SOON

Knowing God in Christ

Our personalities inevitably conform to our god. We have witnessed this down through history. When we worship inferior versions of God. i.e. money, status, security, power, pleasure, you name it – we become like our idols. If your god is money, you will become materialistic. If your god is sex, you will become increasingly sensual. If your god is yourself, you will become more self-focused.

So, this book answers questions like: What is the real nature of God? Is He harsh, as viewed through many Old Testament instances, or is He meek, loving, and gentle of heart, as Jesus portrays? Get ready for a journey into the very heart of the Father, Son and Holy Spirit. This teaching will challenge most of the misconceptions about the being and nature of God. You will be left with a much accurate understanding of who God is, who you are and how you fit in the romance of the ages.

The Void II

The saga continues as life pulls these friends apart, in the midst of dealing with tragedy and the trauma arising from their individual choices and the battle to fill the Void within.